Kittens!
Why Do *They Do What They Do?*

Real Answers to the Curious Things Kittens Do
with training tips

By Penelope Milne
Illustrations by Buck Jones

BOWTIE™
P R E S S

A DIVISION OF FANCY PUBLICATIONS

Ruth Strother, Project Manager
Nick Clemente, Special Consultant
Amy Fox, Editor
J. J. Smith-Moore, Designer
Michael Vincent Capozzi, Cover Design

Library of Congress Cataloging-in-Publication Data

Milne, Penelope, 1960-
  Kittens! : why do they do what they do? / by Penelope Milne ;
illustrations by Buck Jones.
     p. cm.
  ISBN 1-889540-59-5 (pbk. : alk. paper)
  1. Kittens--Behavior--Miscellanea. I. Title.
  SF446.5 .M575 2000
  636.8'07--dc21
                    00-009176

BOWTIE™
P R E S S

A DIVISION OF FANCY PUBLICATIONS
3 Burroughs
Irvine, California 92618

Printed and Bound in Singapore
10 9 8 7 6 5 4 3 2 1

Contents

Why Do Kittens Arch Up Their Backs and Bounce?

Kittens do this jump or "bounce" as an invitation. They may also rear, pounce, or sidestep to solicit play. The arch of the back, especially if accompanied by a fluffed-up tail hanging behind the cat in an upside-down U shape, may signal a defensive threat (or in the kitten's case, most likely a pretend threat). The kitten might be saying, *I'm not coming after you, but you better not try to attack me...I'll fight back.*

A kitten displaying this posture might instead be showing fear, but again is more than likely *playing* at being spooked to encourage a littermate (or whoever is playing the littermate role) to chase her.

Why Do Kittens Climb Drapes?

Because they're there?

Kittens have more reasons to climb than not to climb. First, they, like most young, intelligent animals, explore and exploit their environment: kittens in particular acknowledge no boundaries. Second, kittens enjoy the feeling of rough fabric (like that of heavy drapes) under their claws. Third, kittens (and the cats they will become) love high places. High places are warm (heat rises) and safe (they afford a good view of potential dangers, keeping the kitten away from attackers), and, further, high places are good places to hunt for prey such as birds and insects. If you have a multicat household, you may be interested to learn that some animal behaviorists think that cats use occupying high places as a form of dominant behavior. But mostly, kittens climb because it's fun!

Provide your kitten with an alternative to drapes such as a tall scratching/climbing post covered

with sisal or carpet. Supervise your kitten and, if necessary, use a nonphysical punishment such as a squirt of water or a loud noise each time you see him scaling forbidden heights.

Why Do Kittens Suck on People's Arms (and Cheeks and Chins. . .)?

Kittens, especially those who are overbonded to people or who have been weaned early, sometimes attempt to nurse, or suckle, on skin. (They may also try to nurse on another cat or the puzzled but cooperative family dog.) This habit may persist throughout the cat's life but is not usually a serious behavior problem. If the nursing becomes annoying, simply move away every time the kitten initiates it. You may also help redirect the kitten to more active play with a toy.

In some cases, excessive suckling on people or chewing on material may be a sign of anxiety, especially if it occurs in adult cats. If the cat engages in this (or any other behavior) persistently and out of context to such an extent that it is detrimental to the cat or her humans, consult your veterinarian for a referral to an animal behaviorist.

When you consult an animal behaviorist, he or she will take a detailed behavioral history from you and will observe the cat's behavior. The behaviorist may also request or recommend a veterinary examination. Once basic facts have been gathered (to the extent possible), the behaviorist will attempt to arrive at a diagnosis (working with the awareness that behavioral abnormalities do not always fall into neat classifications) and will create and communicate to you a treatment plan. The treatment plan might involve changes in the cat's environment and routines, changes in your responses or "feedback" to the cat, and it might, in some cases, involve a recommendation for medication, too. Behavior modification takes time, so owner, behaviorist, and kitty may all need to put in an effort over several weeks or longer before the problem is resolved.

Why Do Kittens Chase Their Tails?

A kitten will chase anything that moves, even, apparently, if that something is him! Chasing things and other predatory behaviors are hardwired in cats—even baby cats have a robust set of hunting behaviors that they practice and exploit.

Occasionally, though, persistent tail chasing may be a sign of a problem. The cat may be experiencing pain or discomfort or some other medical or behavioral problem. If the kitten seems to be exhibiting enough tail-chasing behavior that it is interfering with his quality of life, ask your veterinarian for advice.

Why Do Kittens Like to Sit on People's Shoulders?

Kittens like people (if they have been well raised), so they like to be close to the interesting smelling and interactive parts of us, such as our faces. Of course, they like to perch up high, regardless of whether that "high place" is us or the bookcase! Also, kittens seem to like to nestle against human necks—probably for the warmth, the soothing sound (to a baby with exquisite hearing) of the blood rushing in our veins, and the good fit of a furry

body to the curve of a human shoulder.

Experts used to think that kittens should be handled as little as possible in their first few weeks of life. We now know that to be a misguided belief. Even a small amount of human input prior to twelve weeks of age can make a big difference to the kitten's later confidence and friendliness. Kittens develop social play starting at three to four weeks. By week twelve or thirteen, they are becoming somewhat more solitary. Daily handling by people during this window of time increases the chances that the kitten will be attracted to and at ease with people.

The longer the "patting" sessions and the greater the number of "patting" sessions and the greater the number of "patters," the more pronounced will be the kitten's affectionate response to people. These effects seem to be present for interactions with other creatures, also—early exposure to other animals such as dogs increases the chance of the kitten being dog-friendly. Early handling also seems to stimulate the rate at which a kitten develops: "handled" kittens open their eyes earlier, leave their nest box earlier, approach strange objects more readily, and investigate them more thoroughly.

Why Do Kittens Claw So Much?

Kittens claw so much mostly because they do everything so much! Kittens are active and reactive babies, who are in motion for most of their waking hours. They race around hyperexcited, uninhibited, claws extended, snagging the couch as they tear across it in a mad rush!

Kittens also claw with more directed purpose. Cats mark territory with a combination of visual marks left by scratching and scent from glands in their footpads. Kittens also scratch while greeting their owners, during play, after eating, and also possibly to reduce stress and frustration when they can't engage in the behavior they really want to engage in.

Additionally, kittens have special nerve cells around their nails that make them sensitive to pressure, suggesting that scratching may be pleasurable for them. And kittens sharpen their nails and remove the outer dead nail covering by clawing.

Do expect your baby cat to act like a cat! He *will* scratch, so give him a satisfying scratching post or scratching board and praise, flatter, and admire him when he uses it. Choose a sturdy sisal or bark scratching post, scent it with catnip spray and place it in an area of the house where the humans hang out. Encourage your kitten to use the post by dangling a toy against it. Once he has clawed the post a few times, the appealing texture will attract him back for repeated use. DO NOT force him to use it by picking up his feet and "showing" him what to do. Kittens hate to be coerced! You may also want to trim your kitten's nails to keep damage to a minimum.

If despite your efforts in "training and trimming" your kitten continues to damage your stuff, consider using Soft Paws, soft acrylic nail caps, available from your veterinarian. Soft Paws nail caps are glued on over your kitten's trimmed nails. The kitten will continue to play and claw, but the soft, rubbery tips will not "slice and dice" as his own little scimitars do! They must be reapplied every four to six weeks, approximately, because the kitten's nails will grow out to such a degree that the nail caps can no longer adhere to them.

Many cat owners face the difficult decision of declawing their cats. This is a surgical procedure, requiring a general anesthetic. There may be significant discomfort and risk of infection after the declaw procedure. (Discuss these issues with your veterinarian. He or she may wish to do a preanesthetic panel to discover if there are any medical conditions that might influence your cat's response to the anesthetic and may prescribe pain medication and antibiotics post-surgery.) Because of the cost of the surgery to cat and owner, declawing is regarded by many as a last resort, rather than a routine procedure, only to be performed to allow a "destructive" cat, for whom all else has failed, to keep his home.

Teach your kitten to enjoy (or at least tolerate) having his nails trimmed. With someone to assist you, handle the kitten's feet gently as you praise him and your assistant hands him food treats. When he is happy to have his feet handled, trim just one nail, using cat claw scissors or fingernail clippers, then praise and reward him. Gradually, over many sessions, build up his tolerance until you can clip all his nails by yourself without a struggle.

Why Do Kittens Knead?

Kneading behavior begins when kittens are nursing from their mother. They push against her belly, on either side of a nipple, alternating feet to encourage the let down of her milk. Kittens retain this behavior in adult life as a response to pleasure such as being stroked.

If your kitten engages in

kneading to such an extent that you feel more "pin-cush-ioned" than flattered, say *Enough* and stand up to end the encounter. After a moment or two, redirect the kitten to play with her toys. The reason for the momentary delay is so the kitten does not associate kneading you with being rewarded with her toy.

Why Do Kittens Eat Bugs?

Why not? Bugs are prey after all, and kittens are baby predators, practicing to be the incredibly competent killers that they will be as adults. Bugs are a good size for a little hunter to practice on, readily available, and so, so tempting! Of course, some bugs (and other small "vermin") could present a risk to the kitten. Spider bites can cause tissue damage, some beetles emit substances that can cause blistering, and so on. In the western United States, an ambitious kitten might take on a scorpion with potentially fatal results.

Killing prey is hardwired in cats, and it is not possible for even the most conscientious owner to supervise his or her kitten all the time, so perfect protection is probably not possible. However, it is wise to keep your kitten as an "inside" pet and to follow normal, safe pest control procedures so that the huntable bug population at your house is kept to reasonable levels. Remember also, if the pest is dangerous to your kitten, it might be dangerous to you too.

Why Do Kittens Play at Night?

Cats have been popularly described as nocturnal, but this is not accurate. Really they are crepuscular, that is, active at dawn and dusk. They are, however, well adapted for hunting and otherwise adventuring in the dark. Especially baby cats, who with their high activity levels are not gonna stop playing just because it's dark out!

Still, most nighttime overactivity is attention-seeking behavior. If your kitten has been alone during the day while the family is at work or school, she may not have been as active as

would be normal for her and may be needy and wild at night.

If your kitten is waking people at night, do not assume

she is hungry and feed her! That will guarantee she will wake you every night! Do not stroke her and talk to her to soothe her—that, too, will reinforce the behavior. Instead try prevention. Ensure that the kitten has a kitty condo to climb and interactive toys to hold her attention (at least some of it) during the day. In the evening, play with her actively (retrieving, kitty fishing, etc.) and then allow her a cooldown period before you go to sleep. In some cases, getting another cat to play with your kitten may help.

Why Do Kittens Know How to Use the Litter Box?

Kittens naturally start to move away from the nest box and use a dry substrate for elimination by the age of about five weeks, about the time that their mother is weaning them and bringing home prey for them to practice on and eat. They can and do learn both by observation(?) and by trial and error, but litter use (or more accurately, the using of a dry material as a substrate for elimination) seems to be hard-wired in cats, just waiting to be activated at the correct time.

Still, kittens can make litter box mistakes. Prevent these by allowing a young kitten access only to a limited area when

he is unsupervised. Confined to his own little place with his food, water, and bedding on one side of the area and his clean litter box on the other, hc will be able to choose his "potty place" correctly. Kittens are fastidious, so if your kitten has the choice of peeing in a litter box next to his food bowl or on a bath mat on the opposite side of the room from his food, he will choose the bath mat, and unfortunately a bad habit may be born!

Help your kitten succeed now, and continue to help him as he matures. Most litter box problems are caused by a fastidious cat's reluctance to use a dirty box! So always change the litter box at least once a day. Don't just remove feces and allow urine to accumulate—clean the box completely but without adding any chemical cleaning odors.

Most cats prefer an unscented, fine sand clumping litter. Make sure that the box is large enough for your kitten as he grows up. Many big male cats have trouble using covered boxes without bumping their heads as they posture to eliminate. If you have multiple cats you should have multiple boxes.

You have a variety of commercially available kitty litter types to chose from:
- Absorbent clay has historically been the most commonly used litter material.
- Clumping sand litters are rapidly becoming the most popular (at least among cats, and they

have been known to influence susceptible humans).

- Litters made from plant material such as pine, cedar, and grass are also available.
- Recycled paper made into pellets can also be used.

Cats are very particular about their litter material. Once they have established a substrate preference, they will not easily change to another material. Most cats seem to prefer the fine clumping sand, but kittens brought up using other products, such as the environmentally sensitive recycled paper products, will use those willingly. If you need to make a change in litter material, do it g-r-a-d-u-a-l-l-y!

Why Do Kittens Bite People's Hands?

Kittens play with people as if we were other kittens. They chase, wrestle with, and bite humans, just as they do one another. Also, in some cases a kitten may bite because she objects to the way she is being handled and is doing her cat-best to put an end to it.

Bites generally occur when a person is playing with or patting the kitten, (especially if patting is prolonged), rather than occurring out of the blue. Try to assess the kitten's body language before interacting with her. If her tail is held upright, and she is greeting you, or if she is calm, ears held forward and purring, patting is safe and enjoyed by both parties. If she is in an energized mood, tail twitching and ears slightly back, do not attempt to touch her. Either let her play with her imaginary friends and goblins, or direct her to play with a toy.

Never physically punish a cat. When the kitten is in a biting mood, any attempt on your part at physical, hands-on control just encourages her wildness and increases your risk. If prevention and redirection have been only partially successful antibite strategies, try using a nonphysical correction such as a noisemaker or a spray of water. If biting is persistent, enlist the assistance of an animal behaviorist. If the kitten's biting is an objection to what you are doing, first ask yourself, *Could I be causing her discomfort?* and *Is it necessary for me to do this?* If it seems appropriate to continue, reintroduce the situation to which the kitten objected, slowly, step-by-step, pairing calm, tolerant behavior on the kitten's part with a treat and quiet praise.

Why Do Kittens Eat Houseplants?

Cats may eat plants because the fiber is good for them (helping to rid them of hair balls), but mostly they enjoy heaving up green vomit, preferably on your favorite rug.

Some plants are toxic, and your kitten will not be able to discriminate safe from dangerous plants, so protect him. Consult your veterinarian for a list of toxic plants. Keep your kitten indoors in a properly kitten-proofed environment. Make sure to provide him with a little pot of grass and/or catnip to munch on. (These plants are available at many pet stores).

Kittens explore their world with foolish (if admirable!) fearlessness. It is up to you to keep your kitten safe and kitten proof your home.

- The single biggest safety precaution for your kitten is to make him an inside cat.
- Prevent escapes or falls by ensuring that windows are screened and doors are kept closed.
- Do close doors carefully! Kittens tend to run through a closing door at the very last second, risking being crushed.
- Check the kitten's whereabouts before turning on the dryer or closing the fridge door. Kittens love to explore warm places, and what self-respecting kitten would avoid the Great Source-of-All-Snacks?
- Check with your vet for a list of poisonous

plants. You may find it is easiest to give the kitten access only to his own pot of cat grass or catnip. Even plants that are not toxic may be irritating to a kitten's GI system.

- Keep your kitten out of the garage where stored fertilizer, antifreeze, and pesticides may pose a risk to him.

- If the litter box must be in the garage, keep all hazardous materials in a closed, locked cupboard. (Cats are good at lifting latches!)

- Keep sewing supplies away from your kitten. The entertainment of chasing the snakelike threads could lead to swallowing the thread, followed by potentially deadly intestinal obstruction.

- Teach children to handle your kitten gently.

Why Do Kittens Hide in Little Spaces?

A kitten deals with stressful or scary situations by hiding, waiting, and watching—ideally from a high, secure place (though any hidey-hole will work). The kitten will gradually reemerge to join the world as her comfort level increases. Of course, hiding in tiny places is so much fun that your kitten may also retreat when she needs a nap or when she just feels like it!

Try giving your kitten a box with a hole cut in the side for viewing, or a paper bag with the top folded down a bit (so the bag stays open). For extra kitty pleasure, put the box up on a shelf, if you can do so safely. As a special treat, occasionally sprinkle catnip in the kitten's hiding spot.

Why Do Kittens Drink with Their Tongues?

When kittens are first born they have a line of papillae (tiny projections) along the edges of their tongues to help them grip the nipple securely and get a good vacuum seal to suck. But as they grow, kittens develop papillae all over their tongues and lose the ability to suck. Unable to use a straw or hold a cup to drink, the kitten is forced to use his tongue! He holds his tongue like a little bowl curled up backwards and ladles the water into his mouth, swallowing after every fourth or fifth lap.

Why Do Kittens Groom Each Other?

At first, MomCat is responsible for grooming her kittens. She licks them to clean them, stimulate them, and encourage elimination. Kittens begin grooming themselves and then one another by about three weeks of age. They groom each other for pleasure, for practice (perhaps practicing for the day when they will be MomCats), and as part of social bonding. By six weeks they are quite adept at it. Pairs of cats in households may groom one another even as adults. In fact, the mutual grooming may play a role in keeping their bond strong.

Why Do Kittens Have Sandpaper Kisses?

Kittens' tongues are indeed rough. The surface of their tongues is covered with tiny knobs called papillae. The ones in the center of the kitten's tongue have backward facing "hooks" that allow the cat to hold onto prey, to strip meat from bones, and to groom themselves or others (including their humans) efficiently, if abrasively!

There is a downside to having a sandpaper tongue: the tongue's hooks grip even when the kitten might wish they did not. Kittens grooming themselves wind up swallowing the hair they cannot easily spit out. Eventually, especially for longhaired kittens, a hair ball may develop. Do brush your kitten to remove loose hair, and maintain a parasite control program to reduce the excessive grooming that itchiness might otherwise cause. If your kitten is gagging and throwing up hair, consult your veterinarian. Do not assume that all throwing up of hair is caused by something as common as a hair ball—there are many causes for vomiting. If the veterinarian does diagnose the kitten as having a hair ball, he or she can discuss with you grooming, feeding, and other prevention routines suitable for your kitten.

Worse than hair swallowing is biting at snaky yarn—there's no spitting it out again once it's on that raspy tongue. The reverse barbs on the tongue cause the kitten to pull the yarn farther into his mouth and eventually swallow it. Since kittens are in danger of damage or even death from linear foreign bodies, this cannot be taken lightly. Do keep yarn and thread away from your kitten.

Why Do Kittens Roll and Call Out?

A kitten who is crouching, rolling, and calling might be in pain, but if she is six months old or older and has not yet been spayed, she might be in heat. Cats in heat put on quite a display, yowling for hours on end (Siamese cats are particularly known for their amazing vocals!), affectionately rubbing against people, and rolling on the ground. You may notice that any touch to the base of her tail causes her to crouch with her rump raised and her tail held to one side. She may even tread alternately with her hind legs. If you observe this kind of "weird" behavior, make an appointment with your veterinarian.

If your cat is not spayed, have her spayed as soon as possible to protect her health. Unspayed cats have a dramatically higher risk of mammary cancer than do spayed cats, and they are also at risk for uterine cancer and pyometra. The "spaying" will also protect your peace of mind (no more enduring yowling, no more fending off tomcats!) and help you do your part to prevent pet overpopulation.

Why Do Kittens Ignore Commands?

We humans have not elected to genetically modify cat behavior nearly as much as we have dog behavior, perhaps because cats are small, and because they generally fit into human settings less obtrusively than do dogs, needing less advice and training from us to "get it right." Nonetheless, cats can and do learn from their people. The earlier training is started the better.

Usually, if a kitten is "ignoring" a command, he was either never really taught the command in the first place (many times people just start saying *Come Here* or *Stop It!* as if the kitten could automatically understand the meaning of their words) or the owner has not made it worth the kitten's while to care about the command.

Consequences, not commands, control a cat's behavior. Reward your kitten for behaviors you want to see more of. Reward with something kittens care

about—treats, toys, play. Generally, it is not necessary or appropriate to punish kittens. Instead, structure the environment so that there are few wrong choices to make. If punishment is truly necessary, do use a nonphysical punishment such as making a noise or spraying the kitten with some water when you catch him in the act.

Why Do Kittens Reject Some Food?

Probably too much television, watching those grown-up cats make the big money being picky in commercials! But really, kittens may be picky because they really do have special requirements—they need a diet high in good-quality protein and fat. Also, they are influenced by the scent of the food and will not eat well if, for example, they have an upper respiratory infection in which nasal discharge blocks their nose and ability to smell. It may be the scent factor that is responsible, too, for a kitten's reluctance to eat cold canned food but willingness to eat

the same food after it has been warmed, releasing its scent.

Kittens who grow up eating only one type of food may get locked into it and completely reject food that has a different shape, texture, smell, or taste. Feeding a variety of foods when the kitten is young will help keep her open-minded later.

Why Do Kittens Sniff Then Stare with Their Mouths Partly Open?

This mouth-open gaping action is called the "Flehmen response." Kittens do this when they have discovered a really interesting smell.

While cats do not have quite the incredible sense of smell that dogs do, compared to humans their abilities are impressive. In addition to the normal scenting apparatus of mammals, cats have a secondary scent organ located in the roof of their mouth, the Jacobson's, or vomeronasal, organ that helps the cat recognize and appreciate the splendid odors of the world around him. Encountering a particularly fragrant smell, especially those from body fluids that may be rich in pheromones, the cat will extend his neck, hold his mouth open and wrinkle his upper lip. With his tongue, he pulls microscopic particles from the air and transfers them to the opening of the vomeronasal organ, which then relays chemical information to the hypo-thalamus, a part of the brain.

PENELOPE MILNE is a member of the Association of Pet Dog Trainers and the owner and principal of *DubDubDog* in Laguna Beach, California, where she has spent the last twenty years specializing in kind ways to train animals and their humans. Penny also acts as consultant to veterinary practices and animal welfare groups and leads presentations to kennel clubs, community associations, and other organizations. Born in Scotland, Penny now lives in Laguna Beach with her standard poodle, Colin; two cats, Rupert and Nassau; an elderly bunny, named Beth; and a mixed-breed human, Carroll-Oliver.